What's Your Story?

Tarot Spreads and Journal

MJ CULLINANE

For River, you are forever the light that keeps me on my path

No portion of this book may be reproduced without the artist's permission.
2022 MJ Cullinane

Introduction

Hello!

I created this book to help us uncover our unique story. The following spreads offer an opportunity to obtain an unbiased look at who we are through the lens of the Tarot. Some of the spreads in this book will help you uncover those long-forgotten moments that reside within, festering only to pop up without our knowledge, and the result impacts our decisions and, in turn, our future. Other spreads allow your creative mind to play and conjure new ideas that may lead to new opportunities.

What I love most about the Tarot is it is like a good friend who seems to know us better than ourselves. Like that good friend, it can not predict a definitive future. However, it can offer us a truth to consider and, with that information, make the decisions that will create our future. The Tarot is unbiased and honest and delivers the information you need, not what you want to see.

While creating this book, I started watching the second season of the White Lotus. There is a scene where one of the characters goes to a well-respected tarot reader. The tarot cards reveal a deception, a truth the character does not want to acknowledge. As a result, the character becomes irate and insults the tarot reader. That one scene rang so true. How often have we faced cards that reflect a situation as it truly is only to have us deny it?

The Tarot is going to reveal our strengths as well as our weaknesses. The Tarot is going to show areas of opportunities as well as blocks. Like a good friend, the Tarot will be straightforward and honest, especially when it may hurt the most. For all these reasons, when I am stuck, I make an appointment with one of my decks and devote the time to truly listen to what it has to say.

Getting Started

To get the best results from your Tarot deck, it's best to be in a suitable head space. No one likes to feel rushed, including your higher self and the Tarot. That being said, there is no right or wrong way to do a Tarot reading. This is your reading, and you can do it however works best for you! Here are some suggestions that work best for me, and you might also find them helpful.

Make an appointment. Treat this time as valuable and worthy of an entry in your calendar.

Set the mood by creating a peaceful space that is free from distraction. Turn off or silence your phone. Make yourself a cup of tea, coffee, or whatever helps you feel most relaxed. I like to make myself a special cup of tea that I drink not every day. It makes the experience feel more like an occasion.

Make sure you have a pen handy to jot down notes. It is frustrating when you get a burst of insight, and there is nothing to write it down with! I often find myself asking how in an artist's house, there is not a single pen or pencil to be found!?

Before you begin, clear your mind. Consider saying an opening prayer or engaging in a ritual that helps you feel more connected to the deck's energy. I light candles and incense and take deep breaths until I feel relaxed.

Once you are in a comfortable position, hold the cards and shuffle. Shuffle however you feel most comfortable.

How To Use This Book

Although I created this book with the idea that each spread leads to the next, you do not need to go in order; however, devoting time to the first two spreads before moving on to the others may prove beneficial. The first two spreads were created to help build a foundation. In the beginning pages, the main character (you) of your story is developed.

There is room to jot down the card you pull and the thoughts, ideas, and insights that arise. You might find it interesting to go through the book once it is complete and look for areas where the same card or energy repeats itself.

There are additional blank pages for your to write or draw. In the back of the book, you will also find a quick reference guide for each Tarot card.

May your joys be as deep as the ocean. Your troubles as light
as its foam. And may you find sweet peace of mind. Wherever
you may roam.
Irish Proverb

Getting to Know You!

This spread opens the door to getting to know you. Your past, that pivotal time of growth, your strengths, how you tackle adversity, and your legacy.

Cards 1-4 represent the experiences that serve as your roots. You grew from these experiences in one way or another. Pull four cards and for each, check in with yourself. Does the energy/message unlock a memory or experience?

Card 1.

Card 2.

Card 3.

Card 4.

Card 5 represents a pivotal time in your life. It was here that you may have experienced a significant growth spurt, shake-up, or life-changing experience. Write down the feelings and memories that surface. How is your life different today as a result of this change?

Card 6 represents an area of vulnerability, a side of yourself that you prefer to keep private or share sparingly with others. This may represent a weakness or a passion you are not quite ready to share with the world due to a fear of how you may be received.

CARD 7 REPRESENTS SOMETHING THAT DISTRACTS YOU. WHAT CALLS YOUR ATTENTION AWAY FROM A SITUATION THAT WOULD BENEFIT FROM YOUR TIME AND ENERGY?

CARD 8 REPRESENTS YOUR STRENGTHS. WHERE ARE YOU MOST POWERFUL? WHAT BRINGS OUT YOUR CONFIDENCE?

Card 9 represents a point of illumination, that part of yourself that attracts the most attention. Where do you find yourself in the spotlight? In what ways does this energy motivate you? Is it supportive?

Card 10 points to an area of your life that holds the potential of entering a new phase or transition due to decisions or actions made at a subconscious level. Sometimes we spark a change or put into motion events that on the outside seem outside our control, yet in reality, we are the instigators of the change. Are you subconsciously sabotaging yourself? Or moving in a better direction?

Card 11 brings a message of release. There is a belief from your past that has traveled with you since you were a child and has shaped who you are in many ways; however, today, you no longer need to hold on to this belief as it may hinder future growth or cause stagnation.

Card 12 represents your legacy, that which you will give back. The part of yourself that lives on in some way. What do you desire your legacy to be? What seeds will you plant that will inspire and nourish a future generation?

Getting to Know Those Around You!

This spread directs your attention to the relationships that shape your decisions, actions, and growth. Like a garden, our lives are filled with people who make it more beautiful and those who drain our energy and resources.

Card 1. represents true love and friendships. What do they look like to you? Does your chosen card remind you of someone in particular? The energy of this card may represent your ideal partner or the qualities of those you cherish as friends.

Card 2 represents those who are like social butterflies. They are there temporarily but not consistently. What have they taught you over the years? Is there a pattern? Does this energy feel connected to a particular person in your life?

Card 3 brings the perfect partnership. This energy represents someone who is invested in seeing you grow. They not only take pleasure in helping you, but they also benefit from your success and happiness. This card may represent a new love interest or partnership that will be consistent. Do you recognize this energy in someone you know? Where is there the potential for this relationship to manifest in your life?

Card 4 The Weeds. This card brings to your awareness those around you who steal the spotlight, drain your resources, and suffocate you. We all have weeds in some way or another; they may also appear as energy vampires. This card draws your attention to those who could use some boundaries. This is not to say that all weeds should be removed; however, they need to be identified and controlled in some way; otherwise, they hold can cause quite a mess. Do you recognize the energy of this card as someone in your life who drains you? What boundaries could you set to keep the relationship without allowing it to take over your life?

The Beach

The long rolling waves and salty beach air makes the beach a fantastic place to go when you need to clear your mind, contemplate your long-term goals, and connect with your inner child. The beach can also be a source of friction, as anyone who has experienced sand in a bathing suit can attest.

Card 1. Imagine standing at the water's edge as the waves gently crash against your ankles. You can feel the water pull back, taking a little sand from under your feet. As you look at the horizon line, you see the rising sun. You are experiencing the start of a new day. A new day that holds potential. The first card you draw represents that potential. Where is your day going? What kind of day will you have? What energy does this new day hold?

Separately, in a few short sentences, describe your perfect day? Is there any cross-over between card one and your ideal day?

Card 2. As you look out across the water, you notice dark clouds forming. These hold the potential for a storm. It may be a quick sprinkle where the clouds look worse from a distance, or it may be that something significant is approaching, and the time to take cover is drawing near. What energy does your card possess? What kind of storm do you see coming? Is there a volatile situation on the horizon that holds the potential to be disruptive?

Card 3. Brings a dolphin who pays no attention to the storm as it continues to play. This card represents your inner child, that part of you that can find the time for fun regardless of the situation. The card here represents an area where you feel free. This also may describe a situation where your inner child ignores a task because it would rather do something enjoyable. Does this energy help you overcome a stressful situation? Are you blissfully ignorant, or do you just know how not to sweat the small stuff? What is the result of not taking the approaching storm seriously?

Card 4. The Sand; has a potential for friction or, at the very least, a slight annoyance.

The fourth card in this reading directs your awareness to an area with potential conflict. This may manifest as an inner conflict between your inner child, who wants nothing more than to stay at the beach regardless of the approaching storm, and your adult self, who knows it is safer to seek cover. This friction may also stem from how you desire your day to unfold versus how things are progressing due to those storm clouds. What situation holds the most potential for conflict at this time? What can you learn from this experience?

The Night Sky

Staring up at the stars on a crisp, clear night can engage our minds in creative fantasy creation. Although often just fantasies, sometimes ideas are formed, and new possibilities begin as tiny seeds created from stardust.

Cards 1-3 represent the fantasies. Those seemingly out-of-reach dreams would be amazing if somehow they became a reality. Close your eyes and pick three cards. Jot down the card name and the wildest fantasy that could result from the energy held within that card.

Card 1.

Card 2.

Card 3.

Card 4. The moon plays upon fears as it creates shadows and often distorts reality. The fourth card you pull represents those fears. What do you need to see clearly? What holds you back from going after a big dream?

Card 5. Streaking across the sky is a bright comet with a long tail. It is at this moment you receive a bolt of inspiration. What is it?

Card 6. The Crab. With its protective shell and the ability to bury itself deep in the sand, the crab is a master at avoidance. This may be all well and good for the crab, but for us, creating a protective shell or burying our heads in the sand keeps our dreams at bay. What do you need to do to get out of your own way? What is the first step you can take to bring that fantasy closer to becoming a reality today? Crabs don't walk in a straight line; perhaps there is a different approach you need to take?

The Path

Sometimes just having a vague idea of where we are going is enough to help us stay focused on a goal. This spread allows a path to gently unfold, providing just enough information to keep you moving forward without pinning you down to a final destination or purpose.

Card 1. Off in the distance, you see the light and your destination. Where are you going, and how does this place hold the potential for enriching your life?

Card 2. When we embark on a new journey, we often need to leave something behind. This card represents something that is over, something that, although cherished and important thus far in your life, no longer provides what you need while on your new path. What do you need to let go of?

Card 3. Speaks to the wisdom you will gain as a result of traveling down this road. What do you need to learn at this time in your life? Is there a lesson here that seems to repeat every time you get to this point in a new journey?

Card 4.. Bring your awareness to those you may find helpful traveling companions. The path can seem long at times, and having some companionship along the way may prove beneficial. Who is a supportive energy that will help you through the rough patches? Who or what will keep you motivated? You may have yet to meet this new traveling companion. Who is your ideal traveling partner?

The River

There are those times when despite our greatest plans, we get swept up, and before we know it, there is a current taking us in a new direction. This spread was created to help navigate the rapids.

Card 1. Represents something out of your control, yet at the same time, you are being impacted by the events. For example, you have found your dream job; however, a colleague quit, and now you are tasked with picking up the slack. Where is the potential for you to feel out of control of a situation?

Card 2. Points to an area where you are wasting valuable energy. Unlike salmon, humans don't swim upstream very easily. This card highlights what you are fighting against and how this may prove futile. Is it time to go with the flow? Is this a battle you can win, or are you only exhausting yourself further?

Card 3 asks if you are stuck or simply taking some time to plan your next move? The rocks in the river offer relief as they can help you stay out of the water for a little while, but you can't stay there forever. What are you clinging to? What is preventing you from moving forward? What would happen if you let go and allowed events to unfold naturally? Could the river lead to a place of tranquility?

Card 4. is about passion. Has the fire gone out, or is it time to reignite that flame? Your trip in the river may have left you feeling a little soggy, but the choice is yours. Where is your passion? What keeps you going even if it feels like some days you are fighting a current that will not change?

Notes:

The Crow

This spread focuses on how a past relationship holds the potential to impact a future flight path.

Card 1. Represents a relationship from the past that holds a place of significance in your life. This may be a romantic relationship or perhaps a good friend. Although in the past, it was meaningful and played a role in who you are today. Do you recognize this relationship in the card's energy? What did you learn from this time in your life?

Card 2. Shines a light on where your heart is taking you. Did your heart change as a result of this past relationship? What happens when you follow your heart today?

Card 3. Reflects what you are holding onto from this past relationship. Is it a memory or a lesson that has served you well? Or, is this something that requires energy to hang on to it? Energy may be better spent on flying.

Card 4. Focuses on something that keeps us grounded, something that is stable and reliable. What does that look like for you? Is there something or someone who serves as your "rock?"

Notes:

The Hive

Like busy bees, this spread focuses on our working lives, the time that for many of us makes up most of our days!

Card 1. Represents our workplace persona. Is this card in alignment with what you currently do for work? Do you see a difference between who you are at work versus at home?

Card 2. Speaks of the unique skills each of us possesses. What are your talents? Are they being utilized, or are they being wasted?

Card 3.. offers insight into where your talents would be best served. Is this aligned with your current job, or is there a conflict?

Card 4. is all about teamwork. Where is there an opportunity to team up with others so that combined, your talents are even more substantial? Where is the potential for greater success due to teaming up with others?

CARD 5. REVEALS WHERE THERE IS THE OPPORTUNITY FOR SWEET SUCCESS. WHERE DO YOU HOLD THE POTENTIAL FOR ACHIEVING THE DESIRED OUTCOME USING YOUR TALENTS? WHAT CAREER PATH WILL OFFER THE MOST OPPORTUNITIES?

The Old House in the Woods

As you make your way along a lovely hike through the woods, you stumble upon an old house that draws you to its front door. This house was created to help us discover our fears and sources of support.

Card 1. The door opens to an upcoming situation. What waits behind the door is unknown. However, once you cross the threshold, you are committed. What do you fear will greet you on the other side?

Card 2. In the shadows, you get a glimpse of something. What do you see? What is waiting for you on the other side? Does the energy of this card match the energy of your fear?

Card 3. Provides the light switch. The energy of this card will help you better understand what is waiting for you in the house. What do you see when there is light? Does any one thing stand out in the light? Is the monster as scary as you imagined? Can you better understand what is frightening you? How does seeing everything more clearly help you feel more at ease with the situation?

Card 4. Brings a challenger. This energy creates conflict. This card may represent a block or a relationship that needs to be resolved before leaving the house. What is preventing you from tackling your fear? What holds you back from achieving a goal?

Card 5. Opens the door to a room where you will find support. The energy here is loving and kind. You will feel confident and ready to take on any challenge here. Who or what is waiting for you in this room? How will this energy improve your situation?

Card 6. Represents the room in the house with the best view. What do you see? What is waiting for you outside?

The Hidden Room

During your time exploring the old house, you discover several rooms. One was hidden behind a bookcase. This small, musty room has just a couple of picture frames and a journal. As you get closer, paintings manifest within the frames. It is here you get a peek at a past life.

Cards 1 and 2 reveal a past life. The first card shows a portrait of you as a child. What energy did you possess? Can you see yourself? Describe what a day in your life might look like?

Card 1.

Card 2. Is a portrait of you as a mature adult. Who did you grow up to be? What does this energy reveal to you? Do you see a bit of your current life in your past life?

Cards 3-5 are from the journal you find sitting on a table. You discover that you kept a journal of all the critical events in your past life.

Card 3. The entry was written when you were a child in this past life. What significant event impacted your life?

Card 4. Brings an entry from your early adult life. What important event happened? Did it make life easier, or did it make times more difficult?

Card 5. is the last entry in the diary. It is a reflection a life that is closing. What energy did you bring with you when you crossed over?

The Library

The next room you come across is a dusty old library. You can tell a lot about the house's former inhabitants by the books they kept. This spread is a creative exercise, but we learn a lot about ourselves and the books/stories we value. What does your library hold?

For this spread, pull five cards and place them image-side down. Turn over the first card.

Card 1. Looking at the card and reading its energy, what is the first book's title? Is it fiction or non-fiction? What is on the cover? In a few short sentences, what is the book about?

FOR THE REMAINING CARDS, REPEAT THE SAME PROCESS AS THE FIRST CARD.

CARD 2.

CARD 3.

CARD 4.

CARD 5.

The Game Room

The last room of the house you discover is the game room with its collection of glassy-eyed creatures. This spread reveals what seems to be constantly nipping at our heels and what we may never truly conquer.

Card 1. Like a bloodhound hot on the scent of a fox, there is a situation that seems to consistently close in and cause stress just when you get comfortable. What is dogging you? What problem always seems to appear at the wrong time? What is constantly nagging at you or causing you to go into survival mode?

Card 2. The sly fox. Where could you be more clever? Are you missing a weakness in your challenger that you could use to your advantage?

Card 3. The moth is an omen of what is yet to come. How does avoiding or managing the problem impact your future? Is this a problem that simply needs to be managed, something that will not go away (such as a hyper-critical in-law), or is this a situation that requires a solution that brings an end?

Card 4. The stag offers protection. How can you use the energy of this card to protect yourself? What helps you find confidence when confronted by a source of stress or conflict?

Notes:

The Whispering Woods

You find yourself in a dense part of the woods. The wind is blowing through the trees picking up the leaves and swirling them in the air around you. The branches creak and moan as they sway back and forth as filtered light makes its way to the forest floor. When you stop and listen, it sounds as though the woods are whispering to you.

Card 1. Brings a message from the trees. What do you hear? Does it ring true in your ears?

Card 2. You notice young trees pushing their way through in search of light. What area of your life could use some more attention? What needs to be seen?

Card 3. You find yourself focused on one tree to the point the woods seem to disappear. The bark takes on a new look as there is nothing around it to compare it to. What are you hyper-focusing on? Do you need to see the bigger picture?

Card 4. The ax appears because a new path is forming; however, you must make room. The brush will not clear itself. What needs to be removed? What is getting in your way or blocking you from moving forward?

Notes:

The Bridge

Sometimes the path we are on requires us to cross a bridge. The bridge can be narrow and scary! There is no going back; because of this, we need to face whatever challenge meets us.

Card 1. Represents the past, a situation that has come to an end. What do you recognize as being over? What has concluded? What brought you to this place; what wisdom do you take with you on your travels?

Card 2. Represents the troll on the bridge and the thing you must face and conquer to pass. What is required to overcome this fear? What keeps you from progressing?

Card 3. The other side brings new opportunities. What does the future hold once you cross the bridge? Where will you go?

Card 4. Represents a falcon. How can you tame your fears in the future so that you have the confidence to address them head-on instead of flying over them?

Notes:

The Hole

Sometimes things just happen. We think we are traveling along a smooth path, and out of nowhere, we find ourselves falling into a hole.

Card 1. Represents a situation that may be challenging due to a lack of information. You know that something needs to be addressed, yet at the same time, you need to be more open regarding the facts. In what area of your life does this hole appear?

Card 2 represents a distraction that appears to be a solution but needs to be more stable to support your climb out of the hole. What do you depend on too much? Where are you wasting time and energy that could be directed toward a more viable solution?

CARD 3. BRINGS THE SOLUTION, A STURDY BRANCH HOWEVER IT IS SEEMINGLY JUST OUT OF REACH. WHAT DO YOU NEED TO GRASP? WHAT WILL BE THE FINAL SOLUTION TO GETTING YOURSELF FREE?

CARD 4. SHEDS LIGHT ON A PATH TO THAT BRANCH YOU NEED TO REACH. WHERE WILL YOU FIND SOLID SUPPORT? WHO OR WHAT HAS THE POWER TO HELP LIFT YOU UP?

Notes:

The Pond

Do others see us as we see ourselves? The Pond is about reflection, about seeing ourselves from a different perspective.

Card 1. Reveals how you see yourself. What energy does this card hold? Do you recognize yourself in the card? Jot down all the positive and negative attributes you feel represent you.

Card 2. Uncovers how those around you see you. Do they see the real you, or do you create a facade to hide your true self? Do you recognize this energy? How have you displayed this energy to others?

Card 3. Indicates an area of your life where you compare yourself with others. Do you distort your reflection? Does your image seem less clear, smaller, or bigger?

Card 4. Asks that you see yourself through loving and compassionate eyes. What message comes through. What truth do you need to know about yourself that will support your growth?

Notes:

A Mountain out of a Mole Hill

From time to time, we all do this; we make some problem far more significant, more complicated, and at times more expensive than it needs to be! This spread is about getting to the root of a problem that should have been easy peasy but has become an ordeal.

Card 1. Your personal mountain. This problem should have been tackled long ago but now it feels massive and insurmountable. Where did this problem start? How did it get so big?

Card 2. Points to an area of distraction, a place where you find procrastination far more stimulating. Where is your head up in the clouds? What are you avoiding?

Card 3. Look at that happy mole - it doesn't have a care in the world! What do you need to do to shrink that problem down to size? What have you been blind to?

Card 4. Offers a look at what you have the time and resources to explore now that you are no longer blocked by that mountain. What opens up for you?

Notes:

The Mighty Mushroom

Mushrooms aren't a vegetable, and they aren't an animal, no the fascinating fungi are their own category and one our planet needs to keep balance and life moving. This spread honors the vital role fungi play in the life cycle.

Card 1. Like a decaying log, something is breaking down to make room for a new possibility. This may be a relationship that is evolving. You might find your job no longer looks like it did when you started, and the opportunities within that job have dwindled. What area of your life has begun a transformation process?

Card 2. Offers an opportunity to repurpose. Although appearing different today, a situation from your past has the potential to grow into something beneficial or a new opportunity. What is coming back with more positive energy and potential?

Card 3. Represents your community. That network of support you give and receive. Trees use mycelium to communicate their needs across a network underground. Together they support each other by transferring water and other nutrients when a plant is in need. Is there an area where you could be supportive? What resources can you share? What resources do you lack, and how can you communicate more efficiently to get the help you need?

Card 4. Like a fungicide, we can slow down or block our transformation. How are you getting in your own way? What are you doing that is slowing down the natural progress of a situation?

Card 5. Offers a look at what the natural process will reveal in time. Although slow to complete, there will be an outcome. What is the result of letting nature take its course?

The Spider Web

For unsuspecting bugs flying through the air, a seemingly invisible spider web can completely upend their plans. We, humans, encounter sticky situations that seem more challenging to get out of the longer we are in them. This spread will help you see the web before you walk into it!

Card 1. Like a spider creating the perfect trap to attract its prey, someone or something may be looking for a way to entangle you. It might be an ultimatum you can't say no to or an enticing job offer that may limit your potential. Where is the most significant risk of losing freedom or potential?

Card 2. Asks if you have given over your heart to the point that you no longer see your situation clearly? What do you need to acknowledge? Where are you in denial?

Card 3. The wasp is a symbol of courage and taking control of your life. What do you need to do to maintain control of your future? What action is required to release yourself from the situation if you feel trapped?

Card 4. Represents the patterns. Do you recognize any current conflict or challenge from another time in your life? What seems to repeat itself over and over? What do you need to do to break a cycle?

Notes:

The Bat

Although not blind and, in fact, have excellent vision, bats do not need keen eyesight to find their food thanks to their extraordinary ability to use echolocation. Like the bat, when we tune in, we, too, can receive and understand the vibrations that will lead to the desired outcome.

Card 1. The Darkness. Knowing which direction to move can be challenging when you need to know what obstacles may be in the way. Where are you in the dark regarding a situation that requires your complete understanding to move forward?

Card 2. The Moon. The moon's light creates a glow but doesn't illuminate; in the shadows, things may appear differently than they are in reality. Sometimes our creative mind fills in the gaps when we need more information. Where is there potential for the facts to be distorted

CARD 3. THE SIGNALS. WHEN YOU FOCUS YOUR ENERGY ON CONNECTING WITH YOUR HIGHER SELF WHAT SIGNALS ARE YOU PICKING UP?

CARD 4. WHICH DIRECTION WILL PROVE TO BE THE SAFEST?

CARD 5. WHICH DIRECTION HOLDS THE GREATEST POTENTIAL FOR DAMAGE OR DISAPPOINTMENT?

Card 6. Which direction leads to wasting time and energy only to end up back where you started?

Card 7. Which direction holds the potential for the greatest reward?

The Well

For anyone who accidentally dropped something down a well or lost something in a sewer grate, there is the feeling of loss followed by regret followed by anger. One thing is sure; for those of us who have experienced the loss of something such as car keys or a wallet due to carelessness, the lesson, although difficult and embarrassing, is not often repeated.

Card 1. Perhaps you were too careless regarding a relationship, or you didn't take your job seriously enough; there is something from your past that you lost that you look back on today with some regret. What has been lost?

Card 2. What was the outcome of this loss? How did you change as a result of this experience?

CARD 3. Sometimes it's not only our carelessness that contributes to a loss; other factors influence the outcome. What contributed to your loss? Are you taking all the blame when it should be shared?

CARD 4. What do you value as a result of this loss from the past? Is there an area of your life that you are devoted to ensuring is safe? What action can you take today to ensure you don't repeat the same mistake?

Notes:

A Bird in a Bush

This spread came to me while taking a walk in my neighborhood. There was a tree filled with little birds. The dense branches made for a cozy, safe resting place on a cold rainy day.

Card 1. Brings the clear sky and reasons to feel optimistic. Sometimes we forget that there are reasons to feel hopeful, especially during challenging times. What do you forget to celebrate? What can you do today that will raise your vibration?

Card 2. Reveals where you will discover a new reason to feel confident. What makes you feel free? What inspires that powerful feeling within of soaring unencumbered?

Card 3. Slipping into survival mode can create a screeching halt to our plans and have us hunkering down until it is safe to emerge. When in survival mode, we don't plan for the future; we just try to get through each day. The third card in this reading reveals the area that holds the most potential for going into survival mode. In what situation do you feel incapable, insecure, or unprepared? How does this impact your growth?

Card 4. What do you need to let go or do to free yourself? How can you turn fear or anxiety into action that will spark a positive shift and, in turn, create new growth opportunities?

NOTES:

Snakeskin

Every time a snake grows, it leaves behind a little bit of itself, making snakes a symbol of transformation and rebirth. Inspired by the Judgment card, this spread offers a path to growth through forgiveness and compassion.

Card 1. Reveals a stuck or stagnant relationship due to an unsettled argument or past hurt that has not been released. What relationship or situation would benefit from offering your forgiveness?

Card 2. Sometimes the hardest person to let off the hook or forgive is ourselves. We are often our worst critics, and the blame we direct inward can have a rippling effect on various areas in our lives. What do you need to accept and forgive within? Where do you need to cut yourself a little slack?

Card 3. The boxed-in heart controls emotions to the point where they are closed off. Nothing is getting in or getting out when your heart is blocked. Where is there a potential block in your heart or grudge that is preventing you from giving and receiving love and compassion?

Card 4.. Reveals what is waiting for you once you open your heart to forgiving and letting go of a situation. What new opportunity will present itself as a result of this growth?

NOTES:

Judgment

The Coffin

Facing our own mortality can be scary, yet it is inevitable. Eventually, we will all experience death; it is a common thread that runs between all living creatures. At some point, we all cease to exist. That is why we must ensure that every moment we have is cherished. This spread explores the life we have lived and the life we have yet to live.

Card 1. Asks you to consider your eulogy. What will those around you say about you once you are gone? Will they remember you for your generosity, or will they share the "war stories" of each encounter with you? Where did you focus your energy during your life that made a lasting impression?

Card 2. When you reflect on your life, what memories do you hold on to the tightest? What significant time in your life do you contemplate with satisfaction and joy? Where do you need to focus your energy today to cultivate more happiness?

Card 3.. reveals the regrets we experience when it is too late. Although not the most pleasant thought, when you are on your deathbed, what will you regret not doing? What area of your life did you not devote enough attention to? Where should you focus your energy today to avoid this regret?

Card 4.. provides a glimpse of the afterlife. What do you see for yourself? Will you face a new challenge or find a time of comfort and ease?

NOTES:

The Caterpillar

Like a caterpillar, we begin our lives with pre-determined needs and desires. Our movement and freedom are limited until we make the necessary changes that will enable us to develop wings. Through transformation, we discover newfound freedom and the ability to explore options that would be out of reach without this change.

Pull three cards and place them face up. Each one holds a look at a potential future life. Which one calls to you the loudest? Is there one you would like to avoid?

Card 1. In a few sentences, describe what this life looks like. Does it bring joy or does this path offer a life of struggle?

Repeat the process for Cards 2 and 3.
Card 2.

Card 3.

Focus your attention on the life you feel offers the greatest potential for freedom to explore new opportunities.

Card 4. Now that you have chosen your path, which direction do you need to begin the transformation process?

Card 5. Asks you to look around and examine your current situation. Where is there the potential for something or someone to block your transformation? What poses the risk of getting in your way?

Card 6. Offers a look at what your life will be like once you move into this new stage. What potential does this new path hold?

Single Card Readings with the Major Arcana

Deck: Crow Tarot

Unlike spreads that require several cards, the single-card reading offers a quick burst of insight.

For these single-card spreads, you will engage with the energy of one of the cards from the Major Arcana. Read the question or questions and draw a single card. What insights come into your mind? Is there some new information that will benefit you at the moment?

Try to do one a day and see what transforms by the end of the month.

THE FOOL

In what area of your life do you need a faith?

Is there an area of your life that you have been careless?

The Magician

What do you need to do to spark a change?
What situation are you relying too much on magic when a practical approach is needed?

THE HIGH PRIESTESS

The universe is sending you signs, where will you be better served holding back and not acting just yet?

How will be closed off or secretive impact your situation?

THE EMPRESS

Can you give new life to? What needs your support?

The Emperor

What situation will require you to be held accountable for your actions?

The Hierophant

How does your culture or religion impact your decisions?
Are traditions preventing your progress?

The Lovers

What beliefs keep you grounded? What are you passionate about?

The Chariot

What situation is moving so quickly you risk losing control?

Strength

Where are you at your strongest?

THE HERMIT

When you quiet your mind, what wisdom come through?

What are you avoiding?

The Wheel of Fortune

What are of your life is on the upswing? Where is good fortune coming in?

Justice

What block or past conflict will need to be resolved before you can move into a new opportunity?

The Hanged Man

How will a current situation benefit from seeing it from a different perspective?

Death

What no longer serves you and needs to be let go?

Temperance

What situation would benefit from finding common ground? Is there an opportunity for harmony?

THE DEVIL

Where in your life do you hold an attachment that may be unhealthy?

THE TOWER

What area of your life is on shaky ground and is at risk of a major shift?

THE STAR

What will soon enter your life that will give you reasons to feel optimistic and hopeful?

The Moon

What situation are you not seeing clearly? Where do you think you know the truth but in reality the information you have is distorted?

THE SUN

WHAT AREA. OF YOUR LIFE ARE YOU FINDING YOURSELF IN THE SPOTLIGHT?

Judgment

What do you need to surrender to the past? Who do you need to forgive?

The World

What is about to come to a successful end? What will give you reason to celebrate?

Single Card: Yes / No / Maybe

To use your Tarot as an oracle simply think of a question that can be answered as a yes or a no. Shuffle the deck while you focus on your query. When you feel that little tug that lets you know the answer is ready to be revealed, draw your card.

The Fool
The Magician
The Empress
The Chariot
Strength
The Star
The Sun
The World

Ace of Wands	Ace of Cups	Ace of Pentacles
Three of Wands	Two of Cups	Three of Pentacles
Four of Wands	Three of Cups	Nine of Pentacles
Six of Wands	Nine of Cups	Ten of Pentacles
Eight of Wands	Ten of Cups	Page of Pentacles
Page of Wands	Queen of Cups	Knight of Pentacles
Knight of Wands		Queen of Pentacles
Queen of Wands	Ace of Swords	King of Pentacles
King of Wands	Six of Swords	
	Page of Swords	
	Queen of Swords	

The Emperor
The Hierophant
The Hanged Man
Death
The Devil
The Tower
Seven of Wands
Ten of Wands
Five of Cups

Eight of Swords
Nine of Swords
Ten of Swords
King of Swords

Two of Swords
Three of Swords
Five of Swords
Seven of Swords

Four of Pentacles
Five of Pentacles
Six of Pentacles

The High Priestess
The Lovers
The Hermit
The Wheel of Fortune
Justice
Temperance
The Moon
Judgment

Two of Wands
Five of Wands
Nine of Wands
Four of Cups
Six of Cups
Seven of Cups

Eight of Cups
Page of Cups
Knight of Cups
King of Cups
Four of Swords
Knight of Swords

Two of Pentacles
Seven of Pentacles
Eight of Pentacles

Notes

Spellcasting

The key to manifesting is feeling with complete conviction in your heart that your desire isn't just possible; it's also already out there— waiting for you to reach out and grab it. You can wish day and night for a new car, a new job, a boatload of cash, or a new hot romantic partner. Still, unless you believe profoundly that your desire exists and you are worthy of obtaining it—you might as well save your energy. And right there, there is the kicker because all too often, even if we don't admit it, some tiny part of ourselves buried deep down that believes that we don't deserve whatever it is that we want.

Simply wishing, birthday wishes, wishing on a star, making a wish when you see 1111, or whatever sign you connect the Universe to is like calling in a pizza order without actually dialing the number. You aren't going to get pizza; all it does is remind you how much you want it when it doesn't show up in 30 minutes or less.

Tarot cards come in handy when you need to reinforce a positive belief or solidify an intention because they allow suspension of disbelief. Your logical mind won't be fooled into thinking your desire is real without proof, and when you stack the cards in your favor, you trick your rational mind into accepting reality. That being said, you must believe with your heart that the cards are bringing something real, something tangible to you; otherwise, we just fall back to square one.

First things first. What is it you want to manifest? Is it at all realistic? Could you obtain this thing without the help of the all-powerful Universe? Sure, you can try and manifest a rocket to the moon, but really, I mean— really? You would need some serious suspension of disbelief or a connection at NASA to pull that off. However, a new job, a partner who treats you like a god or goddess, a little extra spending money, all those things are available to you right now, with or without the help of the Universe. Getting the Universe involved is to make the process easier. It's like having an extra set of hands when you need to do some heavy lifting. Sure, you could figure out how to get a couch down three flights of stairs alone, but it is much easier when you've got help. First, imagine what your life will be like after you achieve this goal. How do you feel? Are you wearing new clothes? Did you move to a new home? Are you free of the stress that comes from feeling worried about money? Let it all linger around your brain. Also, have fun with this as you create what you want; why limit yourself?

Before you get out the Tarot cards, take some time to write a little thank you note to the Universe that outlines how your life has improved due to the manifestation. I have a "Universe" box that I created years ago. It's basically just a fancy box with a slit on top for depositing letters. I do not open it; it is only for one-way communication with the Universe. Or if you have a fireplace, it is sometimes more satisfying to burn the letter. Watching my words turn into a bright blaze, then poof, off it goes. Either way, my message is being sent, and really that is all that matters here.

Now that we are mentally prepped and ready to go, it is time to get to work! Yep, work, I didn't say it was easy, and the Universe isn't running some sort of charity. It does, however, happily, eagerly, and actively provide for those who take action; of course, the definition of action may vary depending on your goal. Are you asking the Universe metaphorically to move a couch or an entire house? Like a friend, the Universe won't be so thrilled about moving your belongings while you sit on the couch, snacking on chips. Next, pull out twenty-four of the most positive cards related to your desire. For financial matters, you may want to pull out the Magician, Strength, the Wheel of Fortune, the Sun, Six of Wands, King of Wands, Ace of Swords, Ace of Pentacles, Seven of Pentacles, Ten of Pentacles, Page of Pentacles, Queen of Pentacles, King of Pentacles...you get the picture.

Hold the cards and focus your question on what you want to manifest. Keep the question positive. For example, ask if your new job will have opportunities for travel and a bigger salary instead of asking whether you will get a new job. See the difference?

Shuffle the cards and then create a Crow Spread (following these instructions). Because you shuffled the cards and there are more cards than spots, there is a sense of chance, and in that—right there in that randomness, you find the magic. Sure, you could have pulled out the positive cards and placed them where you wanted them, but that doesn't work because it leaves too much room for the rational mind to make excuses for why it isn't possible. Not knowing where each card will land gets our creative minds going.

To manifest a new loving relationship, you may want to pull out cards such as the Empress, the Lovers, the Star, the Sun, Ace of Cups, Two of Cups, Nine of Cups, Ten of Cups, Knight of Cups, Four of Wands, etc.

Let the position for each card sink in.

What card landed in the inner self or heart position? Can you feel the energy that card holds deep in your soul? Direct your attention now to the second position. Can you find examples of that card's energy swirling around you? The third position is the energy that our subconscious mind conjures up. Although this could reveal blocks in spellcasting, it is here to reinforce a positive belief and offer supportive energy.

Similar to the third card, the fourth card in the hopes and fears position may reveal a hidden fear around your desire that could sabotage your spell. Acknowledge it and focus on resolving the belief so you can move on. The card in the grounding position will prove especially powerful as it will help reinforce your feelings toward your desired outcome. It will be what keeps you motivated.

The lesson in the past will help you realize that your dream is not so out of reach. Think about a time when you achieved a similar goal. It is in the external influences position that you encounter the butterflies in the belly that comes from meeting someone or finding an opportunity that will help you reach your goal.

The last card is the advice/outlook card. Looking pretty good, right? The final step is to look at the spread and believe it to be true! Hold the feeling in your heart and see it in your mind's eye.

What action can you take to get the ball rolling? You may also want to summon up so serious enthusiasm as well as that will send a message out saying, yes, you are ready, yes, you believe this desire of yours is there waiting for you, and yes, you will take the opportunities that will help you achieve that goal. Come to think of it, you should also have the Page of Wands handy.

When it comes to manifesting, it is best to start small and consider each attempt an experiment. The goal is to reinforce the notion that you have the power to attract, and belief is essential.

Happy Manifesting!

Card 1. Represents your heart and the honest emotions you feel—the desire you hold within. Here, you send energy out that is pure of—well heart. This is your beacon, your light that transmits messages to the Universe. When you are operating at a high frequency, this card will tend to be positive and represent a goal in alignment. A negative card may indicate that your mood or frequency is low, so your actions and intentions may be out of alignment.

Card 2. Is your heart. This is the energy you attract due to the messages you send out into the Universe. Can you find a connection between the first and second cards of the reading?

Card 3. An area that may be blocked due to a limiting belief. Where are you sabotaging your success?

Card 4. The area of hopes and fears. What is driving you? What do you hope, or what are you afraid of that is the source of friction?

Card 5. Is your grounding energy. You will find your strength here, that part of yourself that keeps you connected to the earth. For example, if the card you draw is the Ten of Cups, you may find your source of strength comes from being part of a loving family. If the Tower or the Death card appears in this area of the Crow Spread, your power may be that you are adaptable and can let go and face change courageously.

Card 5. Your past.. This card reveals a lesson from your history that may be relevant and holds wisdom for your current situation.

Card 7.. The external influence that will enter your life. This person may end up providing the answers or help you need, or they may end up mucking something up. You can't control what they do; you can only control how you react.

Card 8. The crows travel through the veil to bring you an answer from the Universe. Is it the desired outcome you wished for?

Quick Reference Guide

The Major Arcana

Card	Keywords
0. The Fool	Carefree, Faith, Carelessness
1. The Magician	Magic, Action, Power
2. The High Priestess	Inaction, Intuition, Psychic Abilities
3. The Empress	Fertility, Motherly, Abundance
4. The Emperor	Authority, Fatherly, Accountablilty
5. The Hierophant	Religion, Tradition, Conventional
6. The Lovers	Personal Beliefs, Love, Relationships
7. The Chariot	Speed, Victory, Momentum
8. Strength	Inner-strength, Grace, Soft Touch
9. The Hermit	Recluse, Wisdom, Solitude
10. The Wheel of Fortune	Good Fortune, Positive Changes
11. Justice	Karma, Cause and Effect, Justice
12. The Hanged Man	Delay, Perspective, Sacrifice
13. Death	An Ending, Letting Go, Release
14 Temperance	Moderation, Common Ground
15. The Devil	Addiction, Attachments, Passion
16. The Tower	Change, Destruction
17. The Star	Optimism, Positive Energy, Hope
18. The Moon	Shadows, Distortion, Creativity
19. The Sun	Confidence, Illumination, Positivity
20. Judgement	Rebirth, Forgiveness, Transformation
21. The World	Positive Ending, Success

The Minor Arcana - Wands

Card	Keywords
Ace of Wands	Creative Ideas, New Beginnings
Two of Wands	Originality, Boldness, Power
Three of Wands	Forward Thinking, Long Term Vision
Four of Wands	Celebration, Enthusiasm
Five of Wands	Constant Interruptions, Challenges
Six of Wands	Victory, Inspiring, Triumph
Seven of Wands	Combative, Defensive, Holding Position
Eight of Wands	Declaration, Commitment, Conclusion
Nine of Wands	Boundaries, Reserving Strength
Ten of Wands	Struggling, Burden, Over Extending
Page of Wands	Confidence, Creativity, Passion
Knight of Wands	Risk Taking, Charming, Egotistic
Queen of Wands	Healthy, Loyal, Energetic
King of Wands	Charming, Entrepreneurial, Bold

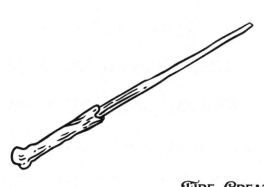

Fire, Creativity, Action

The Minor Arcana - Cups

Card	Keywords
Ace of Cups	Love, Divine Energy, Open-Hearted
Two of Cups	Partnership, Romance, Strength
Three of Cups	Enthusiasm, Friendship, Celebration
Four of Cups	Meditation, Going Inward, Apathy
Five of Cups	Loss, Regret, Sadness
Six of Cups	Nostalgic, Inner-Child, Playfulness
Seven of Cups	Fantasy, Dreaming, Procrastination
Eight of Cups	Closure, Moving On
Nine of Cups	Wishes Fulfilled, Pride, Satisfaction
Ten of Cups	Bliss, Feeling Connected, Family
Page of Cups	Intuition, Kind Hearted, Emotional
Knight of Cups	Charming, Seductive, Unreliable
Queen of Cups	Intuitive, Compassionate
King of Cups	Calming, Diplomatic

Water, Emotions, Intuition

The Minor Arcana - Swords

Card	Keywords
Ace of Swords	Truth, Mental Fortitude
Two of Swords	Fear, Stalemate, Blockage
Three of Swords	Betrayal, Heartache
Four of Swords	Rest, Inner Guidance, Quiet
Five of Swords	Despot, Inconsiderate, Self-Serving
Six of Swords	Travel, Recovery
Seven of Swords	Passing Blame, Deception, Lone Wolf
Eight of Swords	Denial, Trapped, Powerlessness
Nine of Swords	Anxiety, Worry, Guilt
Ten of Swords	Rock Bottom, Victimhood
Page of Swords	Challenge, Truthfulness, Responsibilities
Knight of Swords	Blunt, Swift, Knowledgable
Queen of Swords	Experienced, Witty, Truthful
King of Swords	Fair, Ethical, Knowledgable

Air, Logical Thinking, Truth

The Minor Arcana - Pentacles

Card	Keywords
Ace of Pentacles	Wealth, Practical, New Opportunity
Two of Pentacles	Flexibility, Enjoying Life
Three of Pentacles	Teamwork, Plans, Meeting Goals
Four of Pentacles	Control, Scarcity, Investing
Five of Pentacles	Ill-Health, Financial Loss
Six of Pentacles	Power Balance, Resources
Seven of Pentacles	Assessment, Change in Course
Eight of Pentacles	Apprentice, Mastery, Details
Nine of Pentacles	Affluence, Restraint, Appreciation
Ten of Pentacles	Legacy, Long Term Planning
Page of Pentacles	Trustworthy, Prosperity
Knight of Pentacles	Motivated, Patient, Stubborn
Queen of Pentacles	Giving, Fertile, Resourceful
King of Pentacles	Dependable, Midas-Touch, Generous

Earth, Abundance, Material Possessions

Notes

Made in the USA
Middletown, DE
27 November 2022